The Amazon

Contents

Deborah Chancellor
Character illustrations by Jon Stuart

OXFORD

Amazing Amazon

The Amazon rainforest is one of the great wonders of the natural world. It takes up about 40 per cent of the land in South America. However, this green paradise is shrinking fast and is now seriously endangered.

The world's rainforests

There are lush tropical rainforests in south-east Asia, Australia and central Africa, but the largest rainforest of all is the Amazon.

What is a rainforest?

Tropical rainforests are enormous forests that grow close to the **equator**. The trees in tropical rainforests are extremely tall. They are evergreen, which means that they keep their leaves all through the year. Tropical rainforests are very warm and wet, and provide the perfect living conditions for many animal and plant **species**.

The equator is an imaginary line around the earth.

equator

Venezuela
Guyana
Suriname
Colombia
French Guiana
Ecuador
Peru
Bolivia
Brazil

The Amazon River is the world's largest river.

South America is a huge continent which contains 12 different countries and an area that is governed by France – French Guiana. The Amazon rainforest is found in eight of these countries and French Guiana.

Biggest and best

- The Amazon is the world's biggest rainforest. It is almost as big as Australia.

- The Amazon rainforest covers over 1.2 billion acres. A football pitch is between one and two acres, so that's a lot of football pitches!

- Tropical rainforests around the world are disappearing fast. The Amazon makes up over half of the rainforest that is left.

- Rainforests are good for the **environment**, because they recycle carbon dioxide into oxygen (see page 17).

- The Amazon rainforest produces over one fifth of the oxygen we breathe.

- About one fifth of the Earth's fresh water is found in the Amazon River, and in the many rivers and streams that feed into it.

In the rainforest

Each layer of the rainforest is home to a different group of animals and plants.

Tall trees poking up through the canopy form the *emergent* layer of a rainforest. Powerful birds of prey, such as the harpy eagle, soar above these trees.

The *canopy* is the 'roof' of the rainforest. About 40 metres above ground, the treetops are home to most of the rainforest's animal, bird and insect life.

The *understorey* is just above the forest floor. Climbing plants grow in this layer and big animals, such as jaguars and sloths, also live here.

The *forest floor* is dark and damp. Insects and spiders search for food here, among the rotting fruit and leaves. In heavy rain, a river may burst its banks and flood the forest floor.

Tree of life

Scientists estimate that in just one square kilometre of the Amazon, there are over 75 000 different kinds of trees. Every rainforest tree is home to an incredible number of living creatures. In Peru, one rainforest tree was found to have 43 species of ant living on it.

> Wow! 43 species! That's as many kinds of ant as live in the whole of Great Britain!

More amazing Amazon facts

- More species live in the Amazon than anywhere else on earth.

- The anaconda is the world's heaviest snake.

- The world's biggest rodent lives in the Amazon rainforest. The capybara is related to the guinea pig and is as big as a sheep.

- The golden poison dart frog is the world's most toxic frog. One frog could kill ten adults.

Anaconda

Capybara

Golden poison dart frog

Alive in the Amazon

An ecosystem is a network of living things that share the same **habitat** and rely on each other to survive. The Amazon rainforest is the world's most varied ecosystem. It has the greatest number of different species living in it. Scientists think that over a third of the world's species live in the Amazon. This rich variety of life is called **biodiversity**.

Silver arowana

Species group	Number of known species in the Amazon	Example of species
Insects	2.5 million	Longhorn beetle
Fish	3000	Silver arowana
Birds	1300	Amazilia hummingbird
Mammals	427	Tapir
Amphibians	427	Horned toad
Reptiles	378	Spectacled caiman

Amazilia hummingbird

Tapir

Spectacled caiman

Treasure trove

Scientists working in the Amazon today realize that this rainforest is a treasure trove. For example, lots of modern medicines are made using rainforest plants. Many more medical discoveries may lie hidden in the Amazon rainforest.

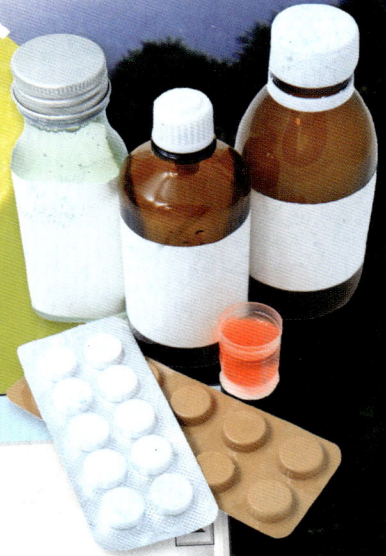

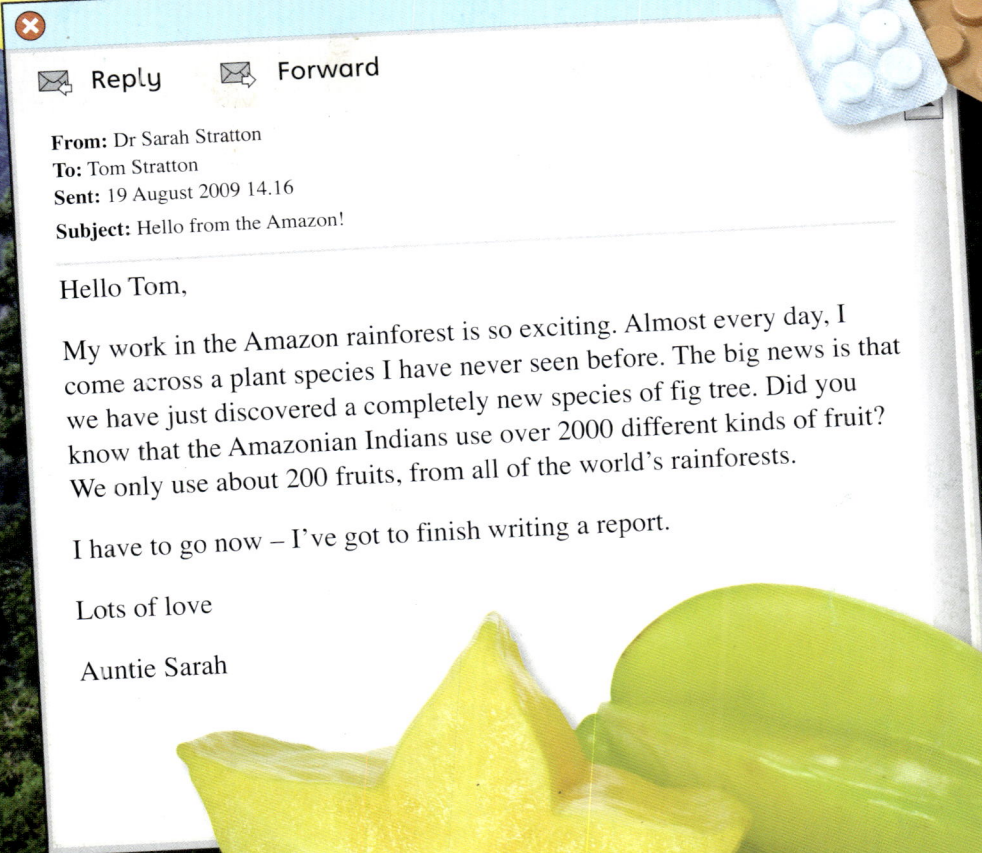

⊗

✉ Reply   ✉ Forward

From: Dr Sarah Stratton
To: Tom Stratton
Sent: 19 August 2009 14.16
Subject: Hello from the Amazon!

Hello Tom,

My work in the Amazon rainforest is so exciting. Almost every day, I come across a plant species I have never seen before. The big news is that we have just discovered a completely new species of fig tree. Did you know that the Amazonian Indians use over 2000 different kinds of fruit? We only use about 200 fruits, from all of the world's rainforests.

I have to go now – I've got to finish writing a report.

Lots of love

Auntie Sarah

Bananas, mangoes, figs, passion fruits and star fruits all grow in the Amazon rainforest.

Discovery!

Most plant and animal species in the world's rainforests have never been studied. In the Amazon, experts think that there are still countless species waiting to be discovered. Expeditions into the heart of the rainforest often return with amazing results. Scientists hit the headlines when they find new species.

A brand new species of ant was discovered in the Amazon in 2008. Officially called *Martialis heureka*, it was nicknamed 'Ant from Mars' because it looks different from any other living ant. It is just three millimetres long, blind and lives underground, preying on other insects.

Martialis heureka – ant from Mars.

I wonder how many more species are yet to be discovered?

A WORLD OF NEW SPECIES

AN expedition to a remote corner of the Amazon rainforest has found 24 animals that were previously unknown. The international team of researchers were delighted with their important discoveries.

"We have found 12 new species of dung beetle, one new species of ant, six new species of fish, four new frogs and one new toad. It is just unbelievable!" said one of the scientists.

Many animal and plant species that live in the Amazon are in danger of extinction, due to the loss of their habitat.

NEW DISCOVERY

Name:
Description:
Habitat:

Atelopus toad
Colourful amphibian
Lives in the north of the Amazon rainforest

Welcome back

Some rainforest species die out before they have even been discovered. This is because their habitat is destroyed when trees are cut down. Sadly, the animals cannot adapt to survive in a new environment. However, sometimes there is good news in the rainforest. Recently, scientists found a species of catfish that they thought was **extinct**. The dwarf suckermouth catfish is now a protected species.

The dwarf suckermouth catfish was 'rediscovered' in a rainforest creek in Suriname. Scientists thought that pollution had made this fish extinct as it hadn't been seen in over 50 years.

In the trees

Toco toucan

The toco toucan lives in the rainforest canopy and is easily recognized. It has a mainly black body and is up to 65 centimetres long, including a bill of about 20 centimetres. Up to 5 or 6 adult toucans sleep together in a tree hole.

It feeds mainly on fruit, but also eats insects, eggs, small birds and lizards. The toco toucan picks and skins fruit with its bill. It feeds during the day and lays 2–4 eggs once a year. It can live for up to 20 years.

Vampire bat

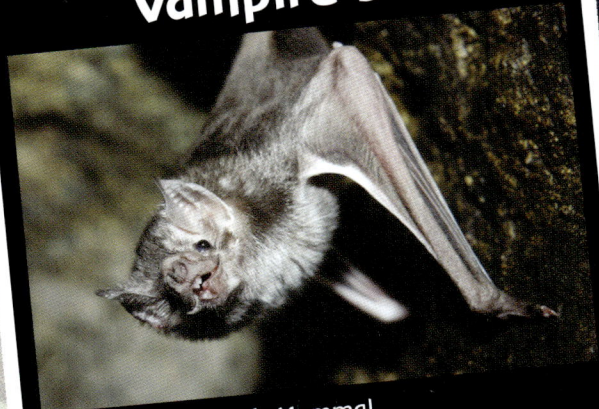

CLASSIFICATION: Mammal
HABITAT: Roosts in caves and tree hollows
APPEARANCE: Grey-brown fur; 7–9 cm long with a wingspan of 18–20 cm
DIET: The blood of other living things
HUNTING STYLE: Climbs onto its victim and bites, lapping up the blood
LIFESPAN: Up to 9 years in the wild
AMAZING FACT: Bats are the only mammals that can fly

Leaf-cutter ant

Leaf-cutter ants are strong insects that live in nests up to 6 metres deep, under the forest floor. There are five different groups in a colony: gardeners, workers, hunters, defenders and a queen. The gardeners are just 1.2 millimetres long and queens measure about 2.5 centimetres long. There are up to 8 million ants in a colony and they live on the fungus that grows from the leaves in their nest. They travel up to 60 metres from their nest to forage for leaves.

Leaf-cutter ants are **nocturnal**. Queens live 10–15 years and, when they die, their colony dies with them.

AMAZING FACT: Leaf-cutter ants have powerful jaws that vibrate up to 1000 times a second.

Leaf-cutter ants can carry up to 20 times their own weight.

Red howler monkey

CLASSIFICATION: Mammal
HABITAT: Rainforest canopy
APPEARANCE: Red-gold fur; males are up to 1.5 m long
DIET: Mainly leaves, but also fruit, flowers, insects and sometimes small animals
HUNTING STYLE: Searches for food in the canopy
LIFESPAN: 15–20 years
AMAZING FACT: The noisiest rainforest species; howls are heard up to 5 km away

Down by the river

Green anaconda

The anaconda is a reptile that lives in swamps and streams. It has a dark green body, with black and yellow spots. It grows up to 9 metres long. The anaconda is usually solitary, but it is sometimes found in groups. It feeds on fish, amphibians, snakes, reptiles and mammals. It hunts in water or hangs from branches to grab prey. When it catches its prey, the anaconda coils around the prey until it suffocates. The anaconda produces up to 40 live young in a litter. Its lifespan is 10–30 years.

Ocelot (aka painted leopard)

CLASSIFICATION: Mammal

HABITAT: Rainforest floor and understorey

APPEARANCE: Light red-brown fur with black spots. Length up to 1.45 m

DIET: Small to medium-sized mammals, birds, amphibians, fish and reptiles

HUNTING STYLE: Pursues prey on the ground, but may swim to catch fish or hunt birds in branches

LIFESPAN: 8–11 years

AMAZING FACT: The artist Salvador Dali kept one as a pet

> Watch out! anacondas spend a lot of time in the water and they are difficult to spot.

AMAZING FACT: The anaconda unhinges its jaws to swallow prey bigger than the width of its mouth!

Red-bellied piranha

The red-bellied piranha is a type of fish that lives in the Amazon river. It has an orange belly, grey back and very sharp teeth set in strong jaws. It grows up to 33 centimetres in length. The red-bellied piranha hunts in shoals of 20–30 fish and they feed on a diet of fish, insects, snails, plants and river animals. They hide in vegetation in order to ambush prey, and they also chase prey and scavenge for food. The younger, smaller fish hunt by day, and the older, bigger fish hunt at dawn and dusk. The female lays a clutch of up to 1000 eggs. Piranhas can live for about 10 years.

Yellow-banded poison dart frog

CLASSIFICATION: Amphibian
HABITAT: Tree roots and wet tree trunks
APPEARANCE: Yellow and black stripes; 3–5 cm long
DIET: Insects, such as ants, termites, beetles and spiders
HUNTING STYLE: Climbs trees using sticky pads on feet, foraging for food
LIFESPAN: 5–7 years (in the wild)
AMAZING FACT: Colombian Choco Indians used poisons from the frog's skin on their hunting darts

AMAZING FACT: A shoal of piranha can reduce a big animal like a tapir (see page 6) to a skeleton in minutes!

Disappearing forest

It has taken only fifty years to destroy over half of the world's rainforests. The rate of destruction is speeding up, not slowing down. Over one fifth of the Amazon rainforest has disappeared so far. Some estimates say that as much as 2000 square kilometres of rainforest is cut down every year.

This graph shows how much of the Brazilian rainforest was destroyed over a period of ten years.

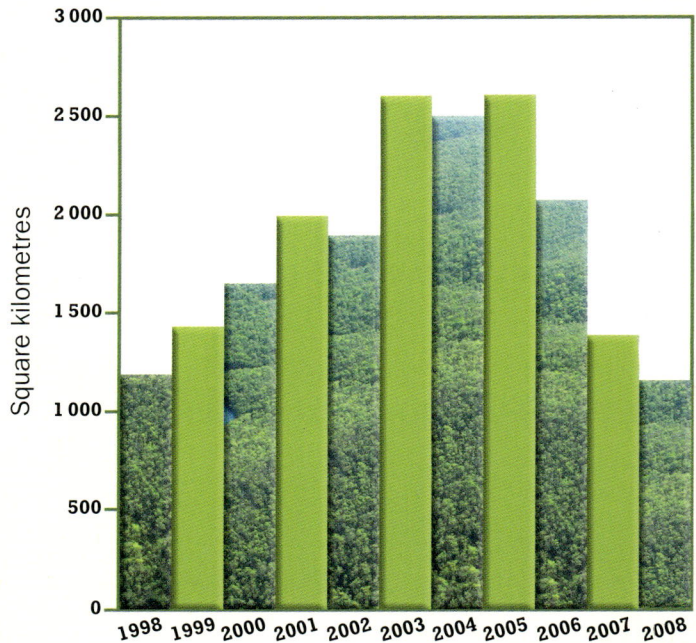

What do you think?

Some people want to save the rainforest, and others want to make money out of it.

I have a family and I need to feed my children. The only way I can do this is to grow soya on the land near my village — and this means cutting down the trees to grow crops.
Farmer who lives in the rainforest

"The Amazon is full of precious **natural resources** – such as plants that produce oil or medicine. More money can be made from harvesting these resources than from cutting down the forest for timber or farming."
Campaigner to save the rainforest

Farming the land

Vast areas of rainforest have been cut down for cattle farms and soya production, so that people around the world can eat.

Timber!

Cutting down trees for timber, fuel or paper is called logging. This is the biggest cause of rainforest destruction. Furniture and paper is made from rainforest wood.

Down the mine

Precious metals and oil are found in the Amazon rainforest. Big areas are cleared, so digging and drilling can happen. Mining in the Amazon causes pollution and damages the environment. Chemicals used to dig for gold can pollute river water.

What's the big deal?

The destruction of the rainforest matters for lots of reasons. Every year, many species become extinct from the world's rainforests. No one knows how many plants have been lost, which might have given us new, nutritious crops or important, life-saving medicines.

Conservation

Pockets of the Amazon rainforest have been turned into **ecological reserves**, where plants and animal species are protected.

In the 1980s, there were only about 3000 hyacinth macaws left in the wild. Today, there are twice this number, thanks to the work of ecological reserves. Volunteer workers help out at many of these reserves.

The hyacinth macaw is one of the world's biggest parrots.

Work at the reserves includes:

- Educating local villagers and tourists staying in the reserve.
- Observing the macaws' habits and diet, etc and monitoring their numbers.
- Working with local landowners to protect nesting sites and create artificial ones.

Global impact

Rainforest destruction is also speeding up climate change. This is because trees soak up carbon dioxide, and fewer trees means there is more carbon dioxide in the **atmosphere**. Carbon dioxide is one of the **greenhouse gases** that trap the sun's rays, increasing temperatures on earth. This is refered to as *global warming*.

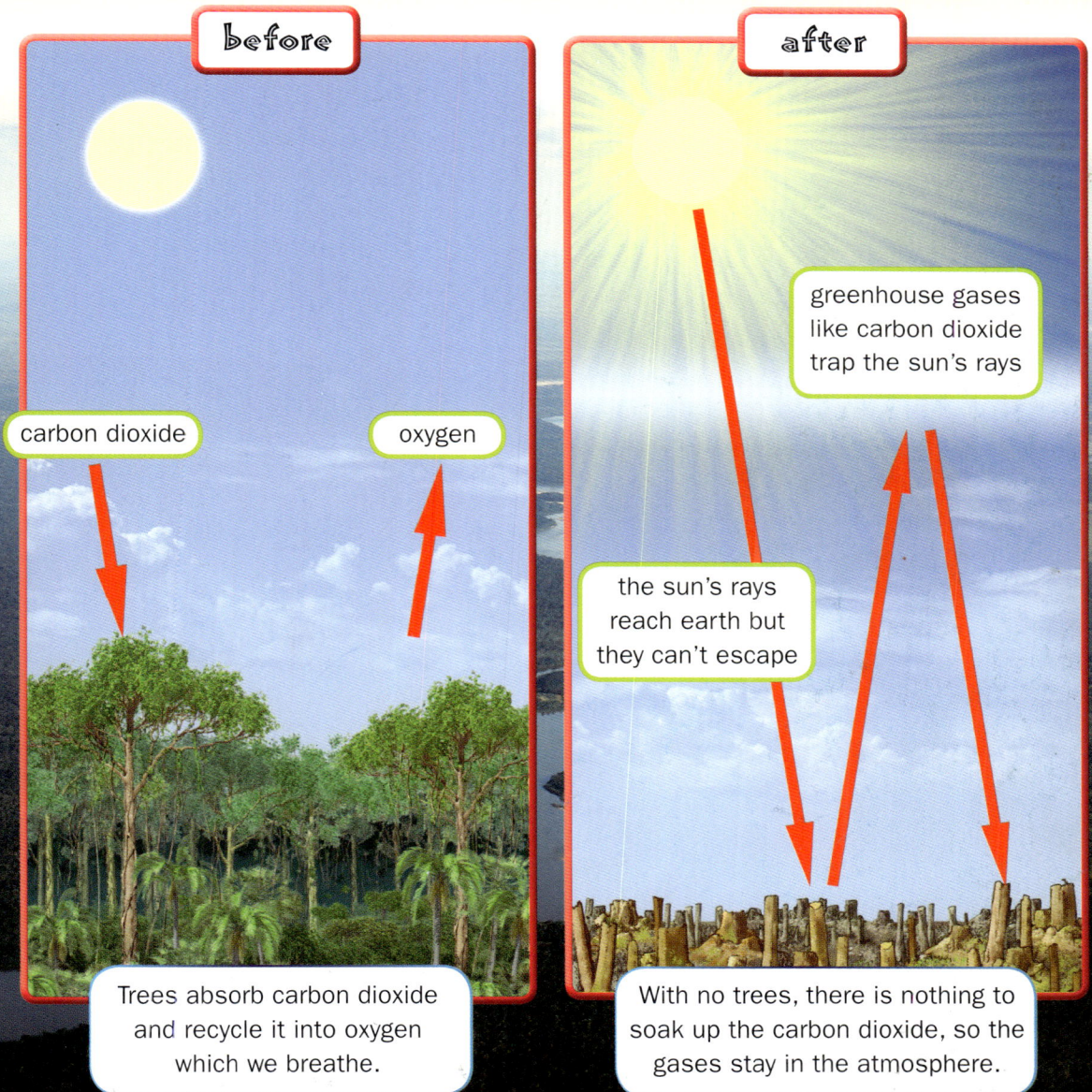

before

carbon dioxide

oxygen

Trees absorb carbon dioxide and recycle it into oxygen which we breathe.

after

greenhouse gases like carbon dioxide trap the sun's rays

the sun's rays reach earth but they can't escape

With no trees, there is nothing to soak up the carbon dioxide, so the gases stay in the atmosphere.

Endangered animals

When a small area of rainforest is cut down, a huge number of living species can be lost. Scientists believe that, around the world, we are losing over 137 different species every day. Many rainforest species are in serious danger – some are very well-known, and others have not even been named yet.

Jaguar

This **predator** has no natural enemies in the Amazon rainforest, but now there are only about 15 000 left in the wild. The main threat to the jaguar is the destruction of its habitat. Many are also hunted for their beautiful fur.

Giant anteater

These strange creatures survive on a diet of tiny ants and termites. They can flick out their long, sticky tongues about 150 times a minute to catch thousands of tasty insects. Sadly, there are only about 5000 giant anteaters left in the wild.

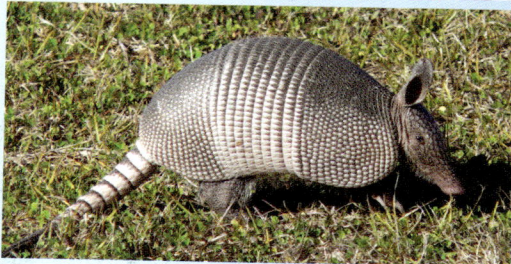

Giant armadillo

The giant armadillo's heavy armour makes it look fierce, but this peaceful mammal has a simple diet of insects. It has been hunted so much, that its numbers have dropped dangerously low.

Giant river otter

The giant river otter is threatened by rainforest destruction and also by overhunting. There are only about 5000 left in their natural habitat.

Black caiman

This species of crocodile was once very common in the Amazon – but in the last hundred years their numbers have been cut by 99 per cent. **Deforestation** and illegal hunting still threaten the black caiman.

Is it too late to save these animals?

No, but time is running out.

Amazonian manatee

This unusual aquatic mammal lives in the Amazon River and is in danger. Numbers of Amazonian manatees are going down due to hunting, dam building and habitat loss. There are probably fewer than 10 000 Amazonian manatees left.

Fight for survival

By the end of the twenty-first century, scientists think that half of the world's living species will have become extinct. If we don't do something to stop the destruction of the rainforest, most of these species will lose their fight for survival.

Up in the canopy

The canopy contains the vast majority of all animal life in the rainforest (see page 4). Many species spend their whole lives up in the trees. They can't adapt to another habitat.

Black spider monkey

The black spider monkey eats lots of fruit and needs large areas of rainforest to survive. It is a 'vulnerable' species, which means it has a one in ten chance of becoming extinct in the next hundred years. To save this monkey, we must save its habitat.

Maned three-toed sloth

This remarkable creature is now only found in small pockets of the rainforest in Brazil. It is 'critically endangered', which means that in the last ten years, its **population** has shrunk by 80 per cent.

When a sloth is injured, it heals very quickly. Studying sloths could help medical scientists.

Blue morpho butterfly

The blue morpho butterfly is one of the world's biggest butterflies, with a wingspan of up to 20 cm. It is also threatened by habitat loss.

Hyacinth macaw

The endangered hyacinth macaw lives in parts of the Amazon that are disappearing fast (see page 16).

Back from the brink

Some rainforest species have been saved from the brink of extinction. In the early 1970s there were fewer than two hundred golden lion tamarins in the wild. **Conservation** organizations worked hard to save these tiny monkeys. There are now over a thousand and the number is slowly rising.

Golden lion tamarins have been bred in zoos and then introduced back into their natural habitat.

Rainforest tribes

The first people settled in the Amazon rainforest about 20 000 years ago. For many centuries the Amazonian Indians lived peaceful lives. Five hundred years ago, there were 10 000 000 Amazonian Indians. Then everything changed. Explorers arrived from Europe, bringing violence, **exploitation** and disease. Tribal people were almost wiped out.

A Paricura girl holds a giant beetle. Amazonian Indians live in harmony with the rainforest.

The people of the rainforest look after their environment. They farm the forest without harming it and only kill the animals they need for food and clothing. As trees are cut down, these people lose their land and their way of life.

Today there are only about 700 000 Amazonian Indians left, although no one knows for certain. There are huge areas of the Amazon that have not been explored and, from time to time, new tribal groups are found. However, it is thought that more than 200 tribes live in the Amazon, talking 180 different languages.

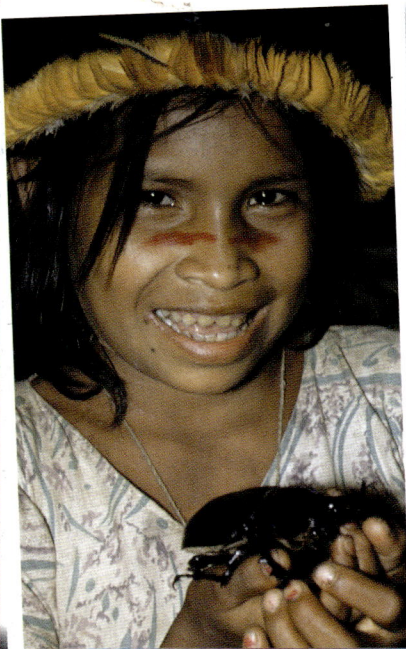

FIRST CONTACT

One of the world's uncontacted tribes has been photographed from the air. The tribe was spotted deep in the Amazon rainforest, in north western Brazil.

The photograph shows a group of Indians outside their thatched huts. Tribal groups like this are threatened by the destruction of the rainforest.

There are many uncontacted tribes around the world. More than half live in the rainforests of Brazil and Peru.

Some organizations fight for the rights of tribal people. Campaigners are working hard to protect the territory of the Amazon's native people. They claim that this is the key to their long-term survival.

Do you think rainforest tribes should be left alone?

Protection zones

Things are beginning to improve for rainforest tribes. Large areas of rainforest have been turned into protected zones or 'reserves'. The people of the rainforest can live in these reserves without fear of losing land to logging or mining companies. They are also protected from unwanted contact with the outside world.

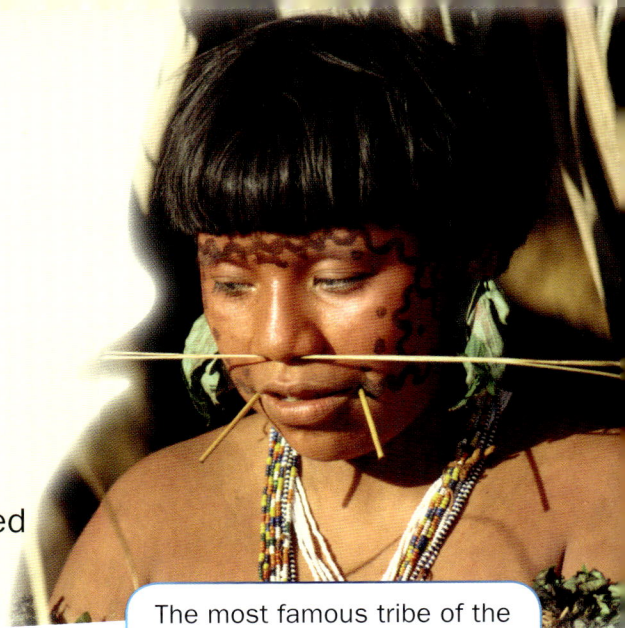

The most famous tribe of the Amazon is the Yanomami. In 1992 the government of Brazil gave the Yanomami an area the size of Scotland.

Ecotourism

Is it a good idea to bring **ecotourism** to the rainforests?

YES
- Ecotourism gives people a chance to have an active and unusual holiday.
- It teaches tourists about the problems that some parts of the world have.
- The money that tourists spend can help the communities they visit.

NO
- Tourists can interrupt the daily life of rainforest tribes.
- Tourists may tempt young people away from the tribes with their 'city' ways.
- Tribal people are often seen as objects of curiosity and may be exploited.

Rainforest industry

Dams are sometimes built across the Amazon River to produce **hydro-electric power**. This makes money and creates jobs. But it can also cause problems for local people and wildlife. There are often big protests against new dam projects.

This is the Itaipu hydro-electric dam in Brazil. Electricity produced at dams like this can provide power for many local towns.

...Points of view

Who do you agree with?

Building dams harms the rainforest. There are cheaper, better ways to make electricity.

Environmental campaigner

Building dams gives thousands of people jobs. It is good for the economy. Without hydro-electric power, there would be power blackouts across the country.

Politician

Fish that migrate down the Amazon, such as the catfish, are threatened when dams are built.

Conservationist

Rainforest tribes have to move to new land to avoid contact with dam workers. When dams are built, we cannot fish in the river anymore.

River dweller

Saving the rainforest

Can we afford to stand back and let the rainforests disappear? If we do, the effects will be felt all around the world. Many scientists believe that global warming will speed up because there will be more carbon dioxide in the atmosphere (see page 17). This will change the patterns of weather around the world, making it impossible to live in some places.

This man is from the Kayapo tribe in Brazil.

Disappearing knowledge

About a quarter of all medicines are made from rainforest plants. When rainforest tribes are wiped out, so is their medical knowledge. One tribe in the Amazon uses over 200 different plants for medical purposes.

How can the rainforest be saved?

Many countries with rainforests are poor and have big populations. They make money from clearing rainforest land.

Richer countries could help them to do the following things instead of cutting down trees:

- trade rainforest products at a fair price
- ban trade in some rainforest products
- plant trees in damaged areas of rainforest
- control logging more carefully
- create more rainforest reserves.

December 4th, 2006

SAFE HAVEN

A huge corridor of land in the Amazon rainforest has been protected, it was announced in Brazil today.

The world's largest tropical forest reserve will be created in the north of the country, in the state of Para. The reserve will cover 150 000 square kilometres, which is an area larger than England.

An environmental group in Brazil called *Imazon* is delighted at the news, claiming that this is the greatest effort in history to create protected areas in tropical forests.

Illegal logging in the Amazon and other rainforests must be stopped.

Is it impossible to save the rainforests?

No, but all countries, rich and poor, must work together to stop them being destroyed.

What can I do?

People are always arguing about the rainforests and what we should do to save them.

Some people think there is not much that we can do. What do you think?

FOR	AGAINST
• If nobody stands up to protect the rainforests, they will disappear in under fifty years.	• The problem of the rainforests is so big, there is nothing that one person can do.
• As rainforests disappear, climate change gets worse.	• The countries where rainforests grow should be responsible for what happens to them.
• More species are becoming extinct today than at any time since the death of the dinosaurs.	• There are more important things to worry about, for example, poverty and war.

Think before you buy

If your family buys furniture, check that the wood comes from a sustainable forest. This is a forest where new seedlings are grown to replace trees that are cut down.
You can ask the shop you are buying from for more information and help.

If you can, choose wood that does not come from a rainforest, for example oak, beech or sycamore.

fact

Mahogany, teak and rosewood are all from rainforest trees.

You can also stop buying food from rainforest areas. For example, check where your soya comes from. In the USA, much of the beef that is used in the fast food industry comes from cattle ranches on South American rainforest land. Always read the labels on food packets.

Did you know
that you can adopt an endangered rainforest animal? You can do this through wildlife and conversation organizations.

Sounds like a great idea!

True or false?

(The answers are on page 32)

1. The Amazon makes up a quarter of the land covered by the world's rainforests.

2. In one square kilometre of the Amazon, there are over 1000 different kinds of tree.

3. Over a third of the world's species live in the Amazon rainforest.

4. Some rainforest species die out before they have been discovered.

5. The red howler monkey can be heard five kilometres away.

6. An anaconda can swallow an elephant whole.

7. The hyacinth macaw of the Amazon is the world's smallest parrot.

8. There are only about 10 000 giant anteaters left in the wild.

9. The canopy contains most of the rainforest's animal life.

10. In 1992, the government of Brazil gave the Yanomami tribe an area of rainforest the size of Scotland.

11. One tribe in the Amazon uses over fifty different plants for medical purposes.

12. More species are becoming extinct now than at any time since the death of the dinosaurs.

Glossary

amphibian	a cold-blooded creature that lives on land but breeds in water e.g. frog, toad, newt
atmosphere	a thick layer of gases around the earth
biodiversity	when lots of different species are in one place
conservation	work to preserve living things
deforestation	the clearing of a forest
ecological reserve	an area of land where animals and plants are protected
ecotourism	educational holidays in undeveloped parts of the world
environment	the world all around us
equator	an imaginary line that runs around the middle of the earth. Countries near the equator are very hot.
exploitation	using or taking advantage of something or someone for selfish reasons
extinct	an animal or plant species that has died out
greenhouse gases	harmful gases that add to the problem of global warming
habitat	the natural home of a living thing
hydro-electric power	electricity made from the pressure of falling water
natural resources	valuable and useful things that are found in nature
nocturnal	awake and active during the night
population	the number of a group of living things
predator	an animal that hunts another animal for food
reptile	a cold-blooded creature with a backbone e.g. snake, lizard, crocodile
species	a kind of living thing

Index

ANSWERS

1. FALSE: It takes up over half of the land covered by the world's rainforests. (see pages 2–3)
2. FALSE: There are over 75 000 kinds of tree in one square kilometre of the Amazon. (see page 5)
3. TRUE: (see page 6)
4. TRUE: (see page 9)
5. TRUE: (see page 11)
6. FALSE: Elephants don't live in the Amazon! But an anaconda can swallow a crocodile whole. (see page 12)
7. FALSE: It's the biggest parrot. (see page 16)
8. FALSE: There are only about 5000 left. (see page 18)
9. TRUE: (see page 20)
10. TRUE: (see page 24)
11. FALSE: It uses over 200 different plants for medicinal purposes. (see page 26)
12. TRUE: (see page 28)